Grade 06
ELECTRONIC KEYBOARD

Pieces & Technical Work for
Trinity College London Exams
from 2019

 Audio access

Published by
Trinity College London Press Ltd
trinitycollege.com

Registered in England
Company no. 09726123

© Copyright 2018 Trinity College London Press Ltd
Third impression, January 2025

All pieces adapted and arranged by Christopher Hussey,
except 'Samba Nights' by Victoria Proudler

Unauthorised photocopying is illegal
No part of this publication may be copied or reproduced in any
form or by any means without the prior permission of the publisher.

Cover image courtesy of Yamaha Music Europe GmbH
Printed in England by Caligraving Ltd

Own interpretation*

Voice(s):
Style(s):
Other info: Fingered on bass chord setting to be used. Left voice is suggested for the LH, changing split point and octave as required.
Bars 8-18 lower stave: suggested use of left hold if available

Celtic Medley

* Candidates should refer to the current syllabus requirements for own interpretation pieces.

Wi' A Hundred Pipers

The Atholl Highlanders

Voices: Xylophone, Flute Ensemble, Trance Synth (or Perc Synth), Dance Synth, 80s Synth (or Synth Brass)
Style: 80s Pop Rock or Trance Pop
Split point: Accomp. E♭3
Other info: Fingered on bass chord setting to be used.
All voices to sound at written pitch using octave transposition as necessary (unless otherwise stated).
Flute Ensemble to sound at written pitch and include octave below, if possible.
Transposition: Bars 6-21 Trance Synth (sound Octave -1), bars 22-37 Dance Synth Octave -1 to be played an octave higher than written
Pitch bend range = 2; Pitch bend (↗ or ↘) to be used where instructed: glide up/down to written note

Flow, My Tears

John Dowland

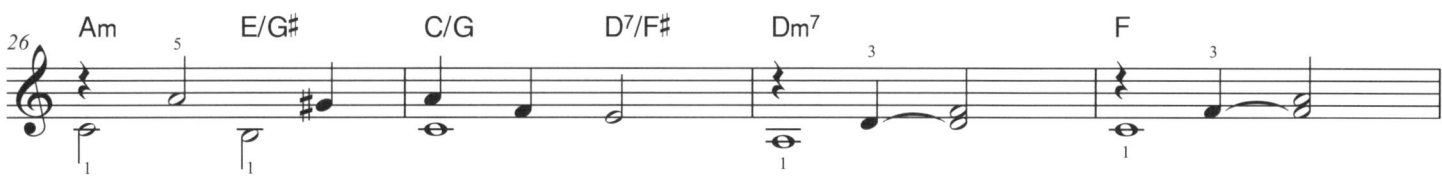

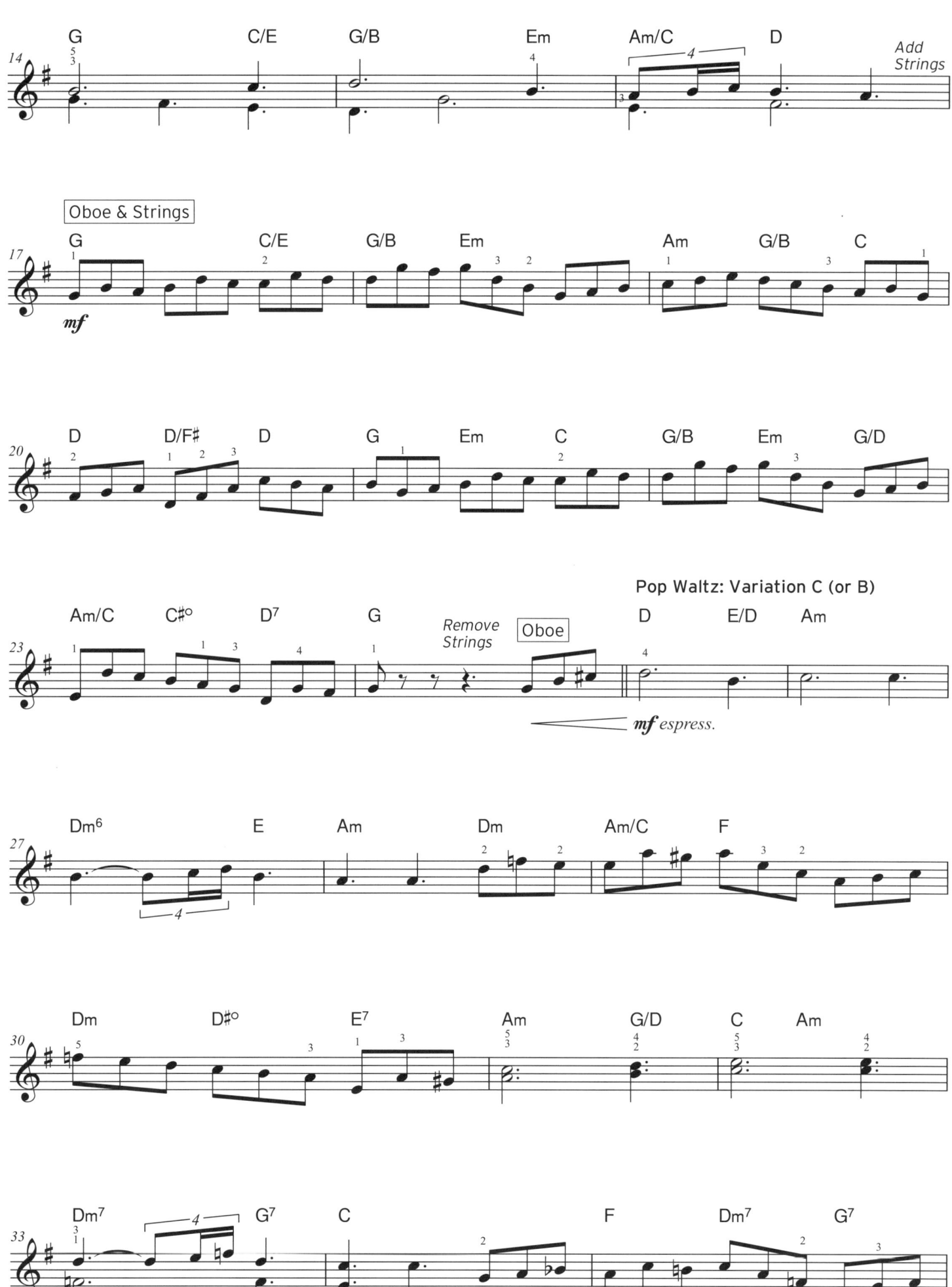

Voices: Warm Strings, Grand Piano, Oboe, Flute, Acoustic Guitar
Style: Piano Ballad
Split point: Accomp. F^3
Other info: Fingered on bass chord setting to be used. All voices to sound at written pitch using octave transposition as necessary (unless otherwise stated).
Transposition is as follows: Bars 1-12 Octave -1 to be played an octave higher than written;
Bars 41-49 Acoustic Guitar to sound an octave lower than written

Romanze

from *Piano Concerto no. 1*, op. 11

Frédéric Chopin

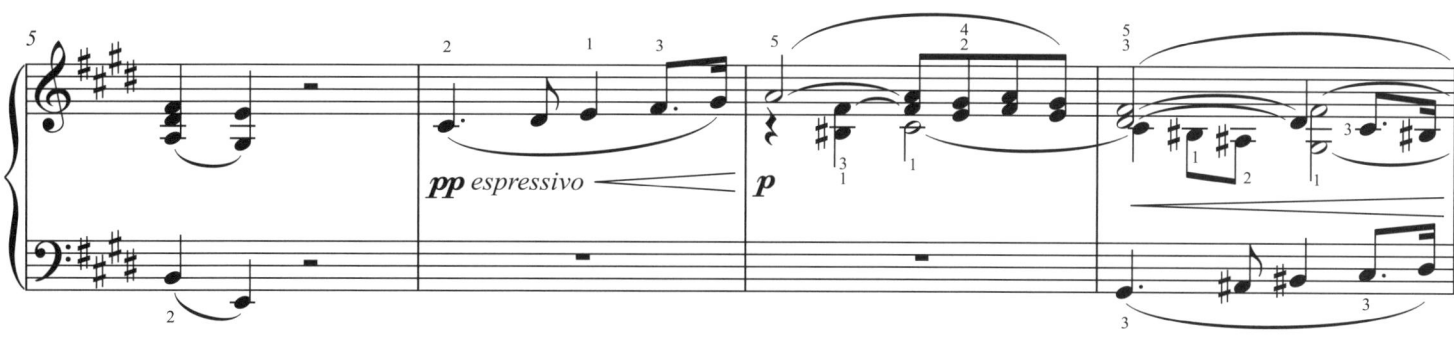

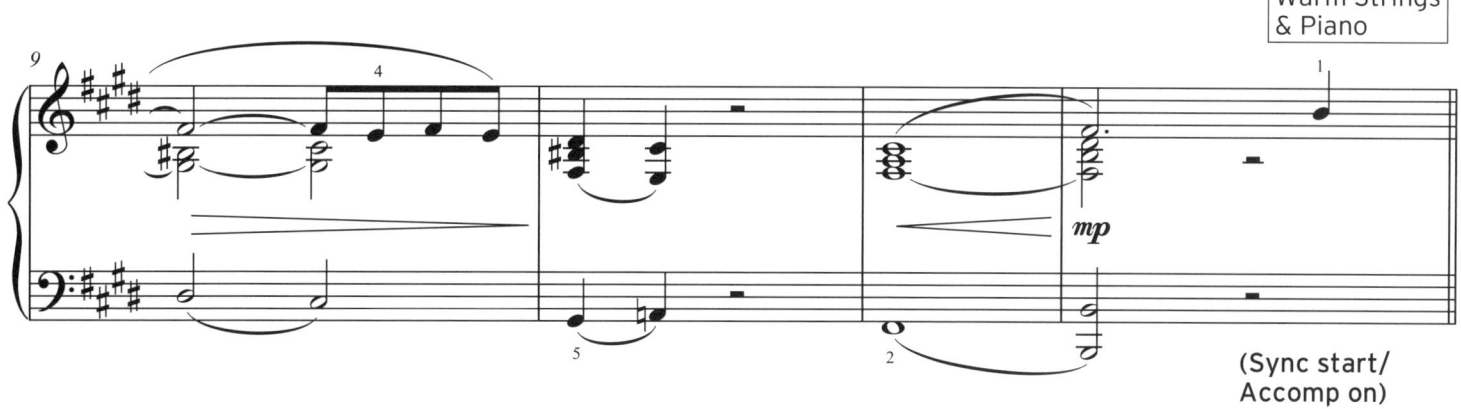

© Copyright 2018 Trinity College London Press Ltd

Voices: Honky-Tonk Piano, Jazz Flute, Jazz Vibraphone, Jazz Guitar, Power Brass (Big Band Brass), Soft Trombones
Style: Fast Jazz, Big Band Swing
Split point: Accomp. B²
Other info: Fingered chord setting to be used. All voices to sound at written pitch (unless otherwise stated).
Transposition is as follows: Vibraphone and Guitar to sound Octave -1 throughout
Pitch bend range = 1; Pitch bend to be used where instructed: ↗ = glide upwards to written notes

King Porter Stomp

Jelly Roll Morton

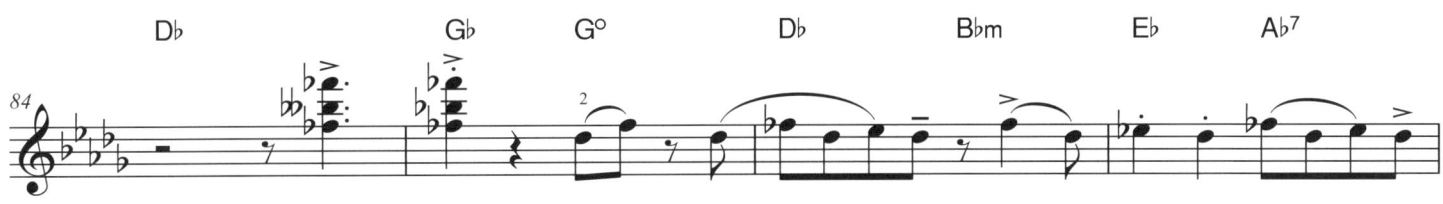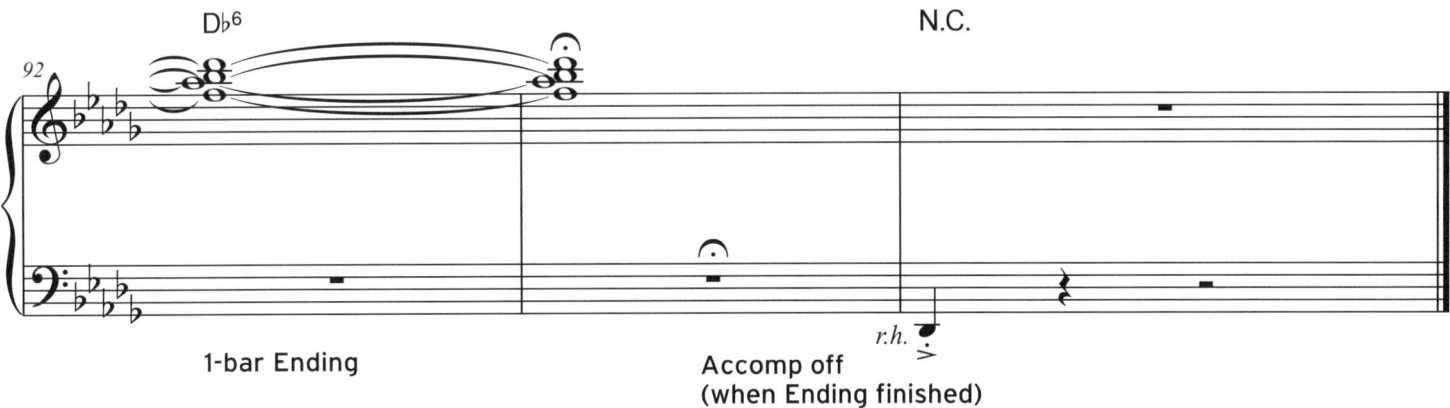

1-bar Ending

Accomp off
(when Ending finished)

Please set up for the next piece

Voices: Alto Flute Ensemble (or Flutes), Flugelhorn (or Trombone), Acoustic Guitar, Tenor Sax, Piano
Style: Bossa Nova
Split point: Accomp. F³ Left Voice F³
Other info: Fingered chord setting to be used. All voices to sound at written pitch using octave transposition as necessary (unless otherwise stated). Flugelhorn, Acoustic Guitar and Tenor Sax to sound octave lower, Piano (Left Voice) to sound two octaves higher.
Transposition is as follows: Bars 24 (last beat)–25 Right Voice -1 octave to be played up an octave,
Bars 50–65 Right Voice to be played an octave higher than written (sounding down an octave),
Bars 50–57 and 66–81 Left Voice to be played two octaves lower than written (sounding two octaves higher).

Girl from Ipanema

Music by Antônio Carlos Jobim
English words by Norman Gimbel
Original words by Vinicius De Moraes

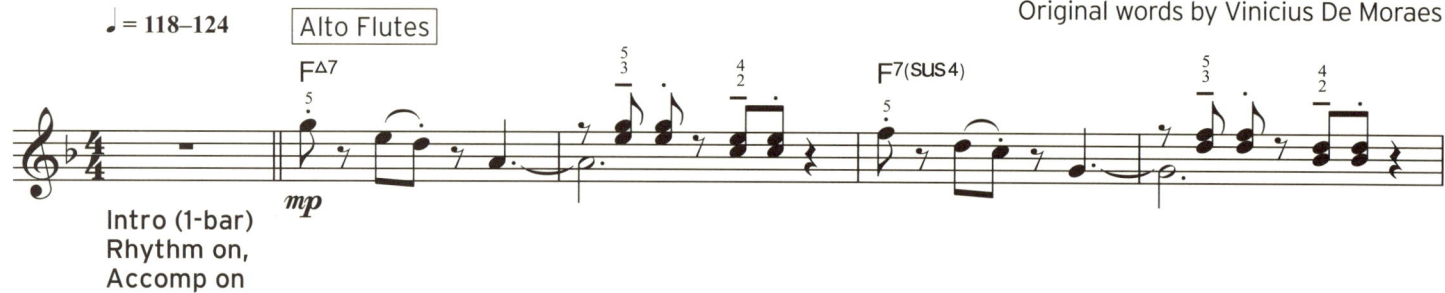

Copyright © 1963 Fox Gimbel Productions/Songs of Universal Inc.
Universal/MCA Music Limited. Rights for Fox Gimbel Productions assigned to Words West.
This arrangement Copyright © 2018 Copyright © 1963 Fox Gimbel Productions/Songs of Universal Inc.
International Copyright Secured. All Rights Reserved. Used by permission of Hal Leonard Europe Limited.

Gm7
Eb7
Remove L.V.
Am7
D7
Gm7
C7
Fill to A
(Flugelhorn sounding octave lower)
Alto Flutes & Flugelhorn
FΔ7
mp
G7
Gm7
Gb7
FΔ7
Gb7
FΔ7
Gb7
FΔ7
Gb7
FΔ7
Ending (1-bar)

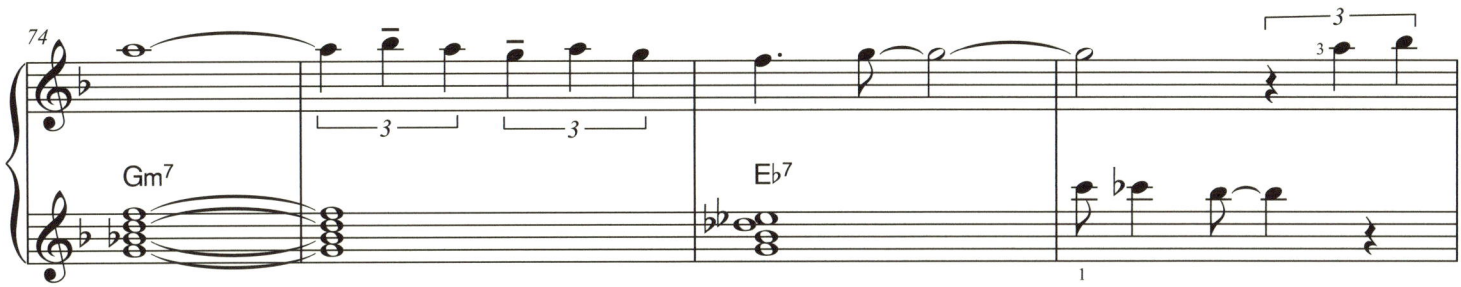

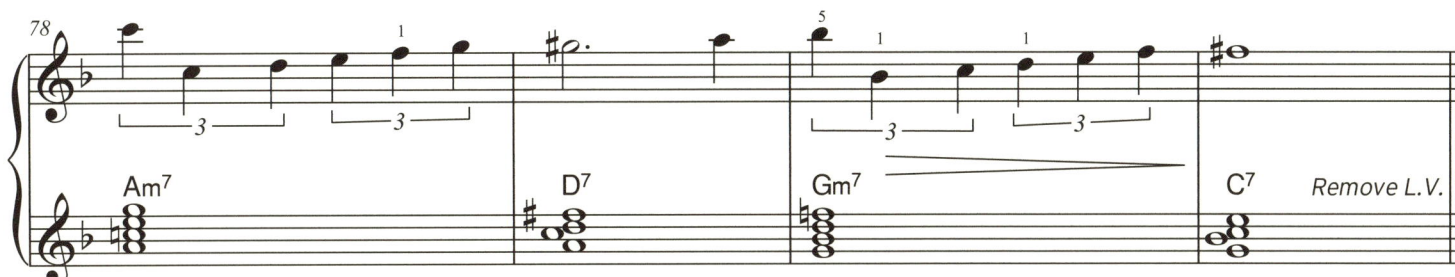

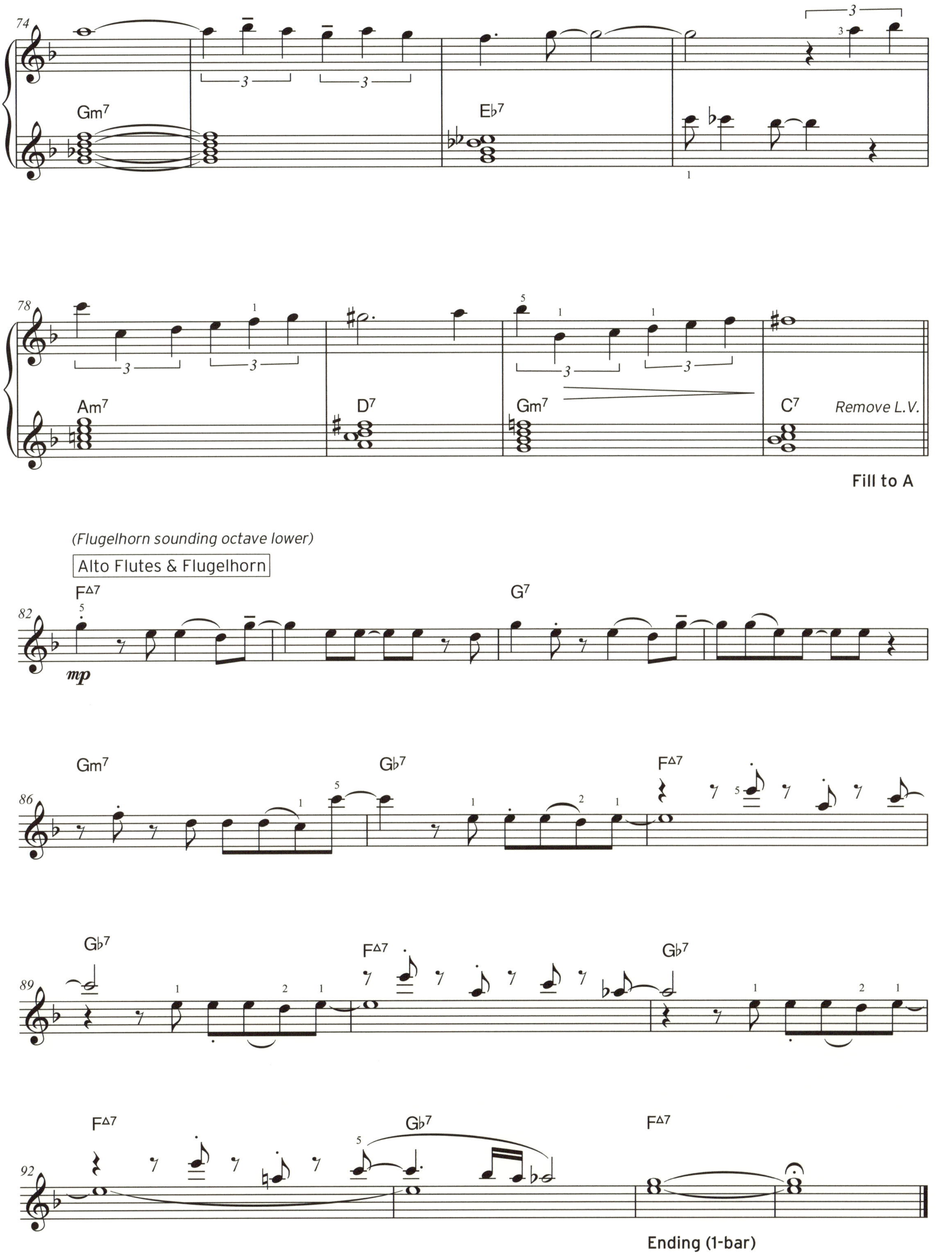

Voices:	Piano, Power Brass, Jazz Flute, Electric Piano, Strings
Style:	*70s Disco Funk*
Split point:	Accomp. Bars 1–6 A♭², 7–end F³, Left Voice Bars 1–6 A♭², 7–end F³
Other info:	Fingered setting to be used. All voices to sound at written pitch using octave transposition as necessary (unless otherwise stated).
	Transposition is as follows: Bars 1–6 Left Voice Octave -1 to be played an octave higher than written, Bars 11–26, 43–58 Left Voice Octave +1 to be played an octave lower than written.

September

Words and Music by Maurice White,
Al McKay and Allee Willis

Copyright © 1978 EMI April Music Inc/Irving Music Inc.
Rights for World excluding USA & Canada administered by EMI Music Publishing Limited and Rondor International Inc.
Rights for USA & Canada administered by Sony/ATV Music Publishing LLC.
This arrangement Copyright © EMI April Music Inc/Irving Music Inc.
International Copyright Secured. All Rights Reserved. Used by permission of Hal Leonard Europe Limited

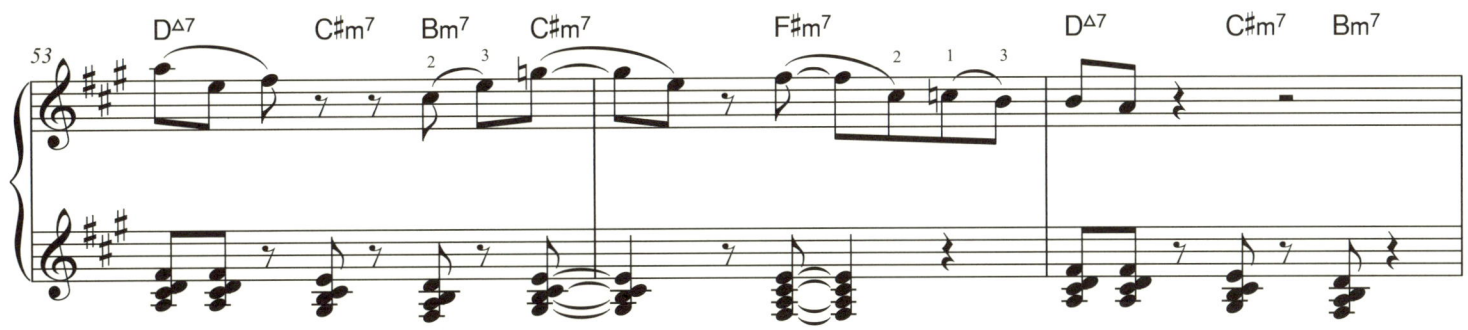
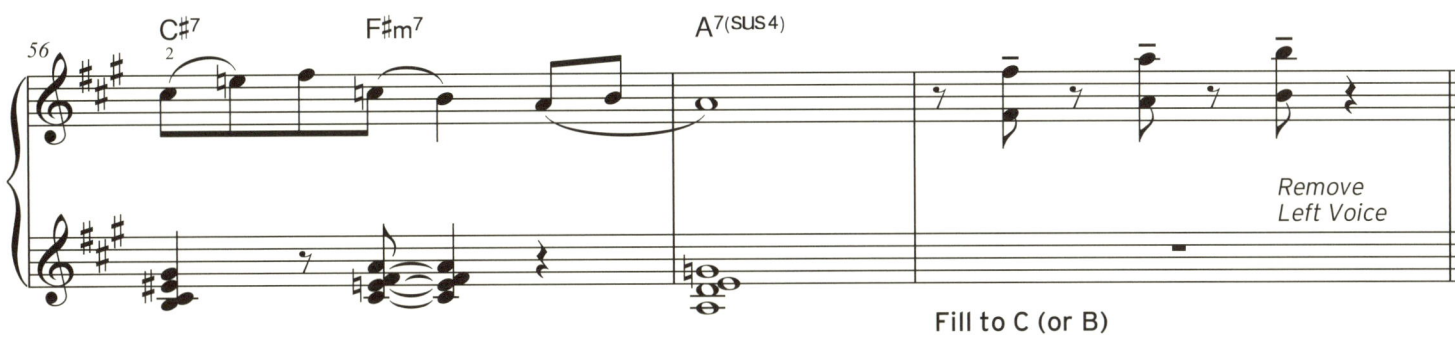

Fill to C (or B)

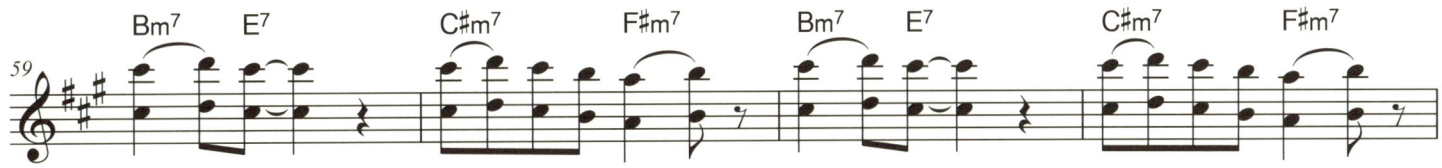

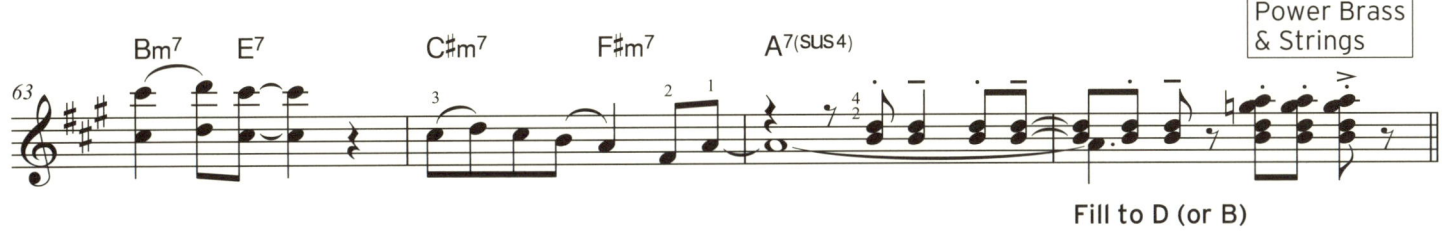

Fill to D (or B)

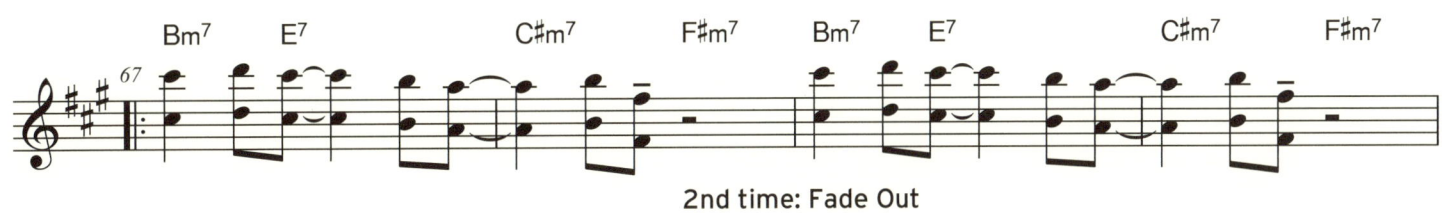

2nd time: Fade Out

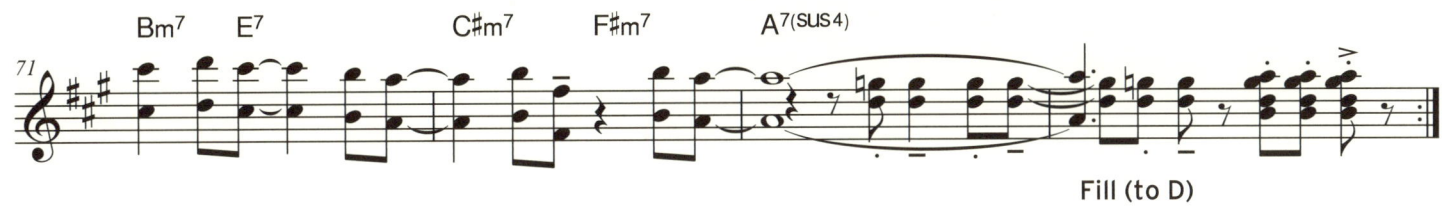

Fill (to D)

Play repeat in the exam

Voices: Guitar (to sound at written pitch), Trumpet, Brass, Flute, Marimba, Piano
Style: Brazillian Samba
Split point: Accomp. bars 1-24 and 57-end F#2. Accomp. and Left Voice bars 25-56 C3
Other info: In bars 25-56, Left Voice chords should be played an octave lower. All voices to sound at written pitch using octave transpose as necessary.

Samba Nights

Victoria Proudler

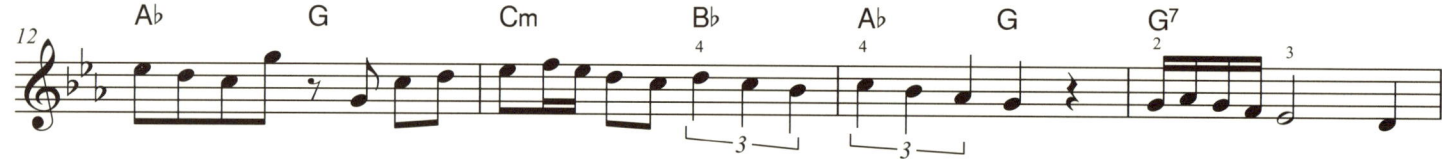

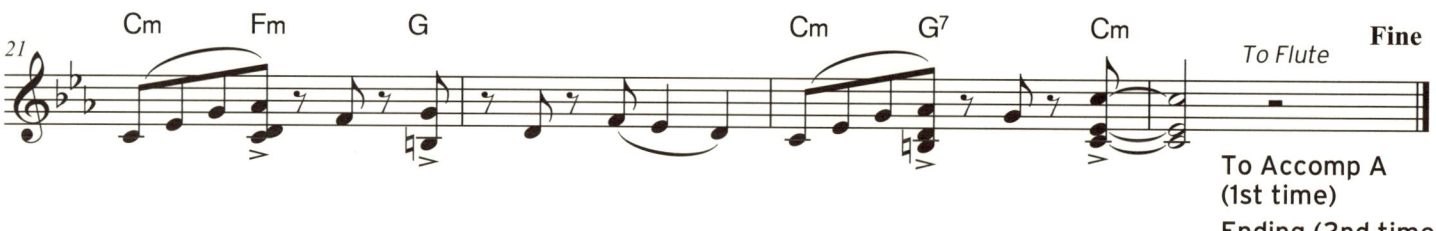

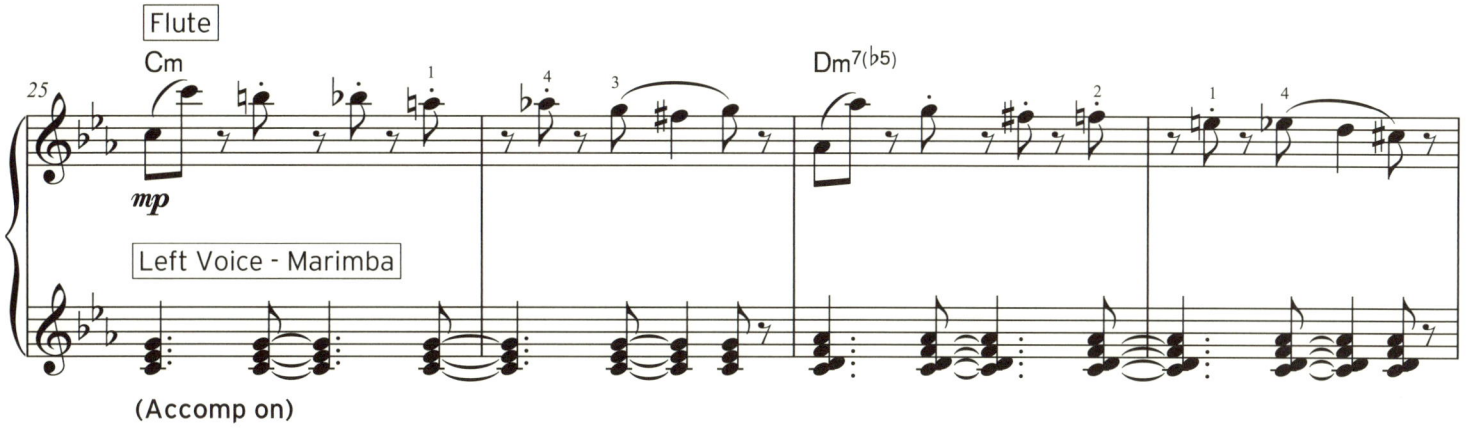
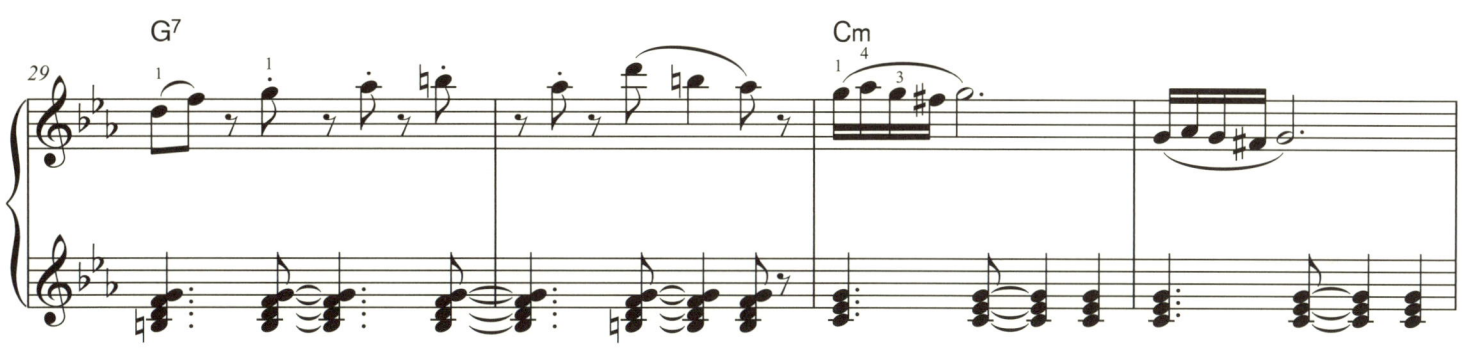
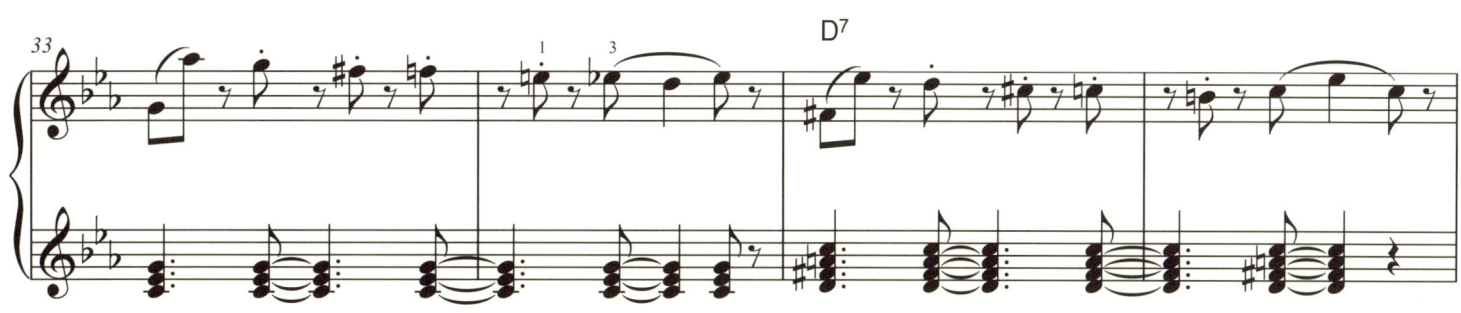
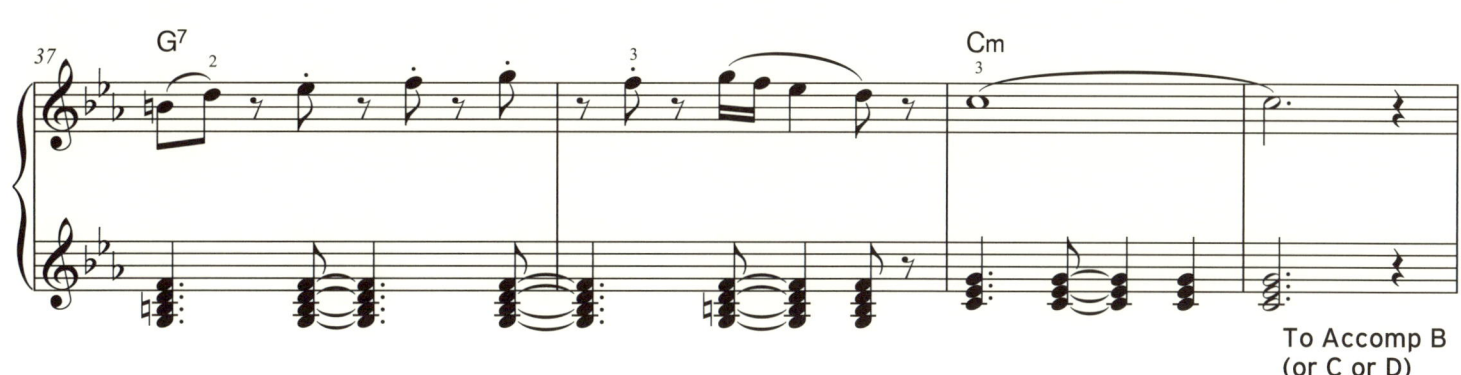

To Accomp B
(or C or D)

Technical work

Candidates prepare section **1.** and *either* section **2.** *or* section **3.**

1. KEYBOARD EXERCISE (from memory)

Candidates should choose *one* of the scale & arpeggio combinations (marked *) in section **2.** below using *one* of the tonal/modal centres of F, D or D♭/C♯ (candidate choice).

Either
2. SCALES & CHORD KNOWLEDGE (from memory) – **Examiners select from the following:**

Using the tonal/modal centres of F, D and D♭/C♯: * Major scale followed by major 7th arpeggio * Dorian scale followed by minor 7th arpeggio * Mixolydian scale followed by major arpeggio with a lowered 7th (F^7, D^7, D♭^{7}) (NB: candidates will not be asked again for whichever scale & arpeggio combination they selected for section **1.**)	scale hands together, arpeggio in RH only	two octaves	*legato* *mf*	min. ♩ = 120
Major pentatonic scale on F, D and D♭	hands separately, straight *or* swung (examiner choice)			
Minor pentatonic scale on F, D and C♯				
Chromatic scale in similar motion starting on any white note (examiner choice)	hands together			
Blues scale on F, D and C♯	RH only, straight *or* swung (examiner choice)			
Chords in root position: F^6, D^6, D♭^{6}, Fm^6, Dm^6, D♭m^6 F^7, D^7, D♭^{7}, C^7, A^7, A♭^{7} F$^{△7}$, D$^{△7}$, D♭$^{△7}$, Fm^7, Dm^7, D♭m^7 F$^{○7}$, D$^{○7}$, D♭$^{○7}$	bass note in LH and remaining notes in RH			

Or
3. EXERCISES (music may be used) – **Candidates prepare three of the following four exercises.**

Candidates choose one exercise to play first. Examiners then select one of the remaining two prepared exercises to be performed.

1.	Eastern Song	keyboard functions exercise
2.	Beguine	scalic exercise
3.	Latin Escapade	pianistic exercise
4.	Fishes' Lament	sequencing exercise

1. Keyboard exercise

Two octave scale, followed by arpeggio

F major scale, major 7th arpeggio

D major scale, major 7th arpeggio

D♭ major scale, major 7th arpeggio

Dorian scale starting on F, minor 7th arpeggio

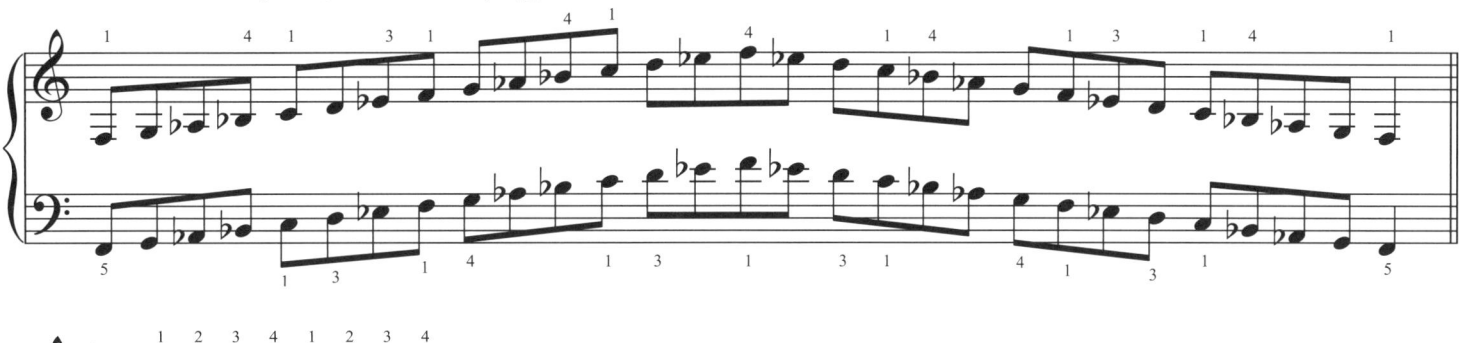
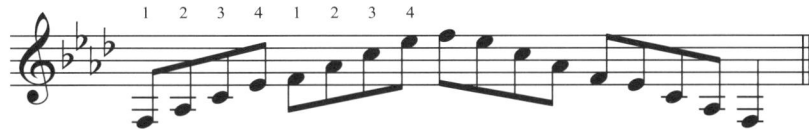

Dorian scale starting on D, minor 7th arpeggio

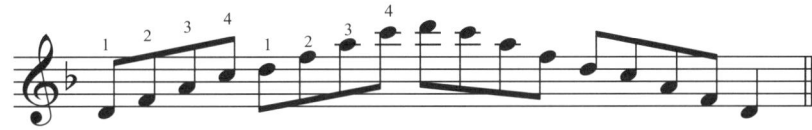

Dorian scale starting on C♯, minor 7th arpeggio

Mixolydian scale starting on F, major arpeggio with lowered 7th

Mixolydian scale starting on D, major arpeggio with lowered 7th

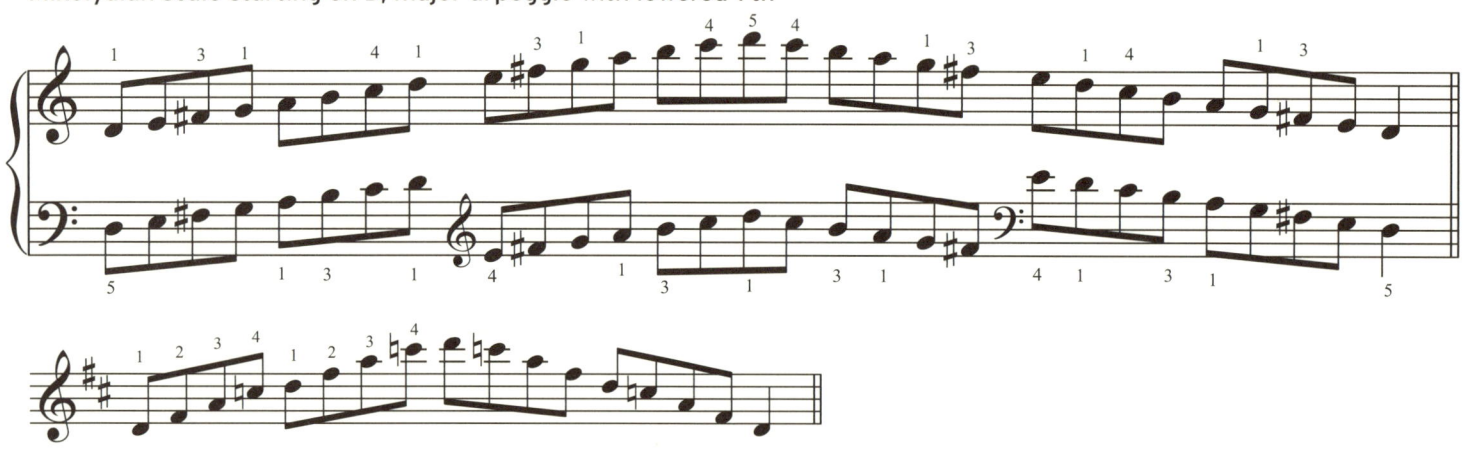

Mixolydian scale starting on D♭, major arpeggio with lowered 7th

2. Scales & chord knowledge

Two octave scale, followed by arpeggio

F major scale, major 7th arpeggio

D major scale, major 7th arpeggio

D♭ major scale, major 7th arpeggio

Dorian scale starting on F, minor 7th arpeggio

Dorian scale starting on D, minor 7th arpeggio

Dorian scale starting on C♯, minor 7th arpeggio

Mixolydian scale starting on F, major arpeggio with lowered 7th

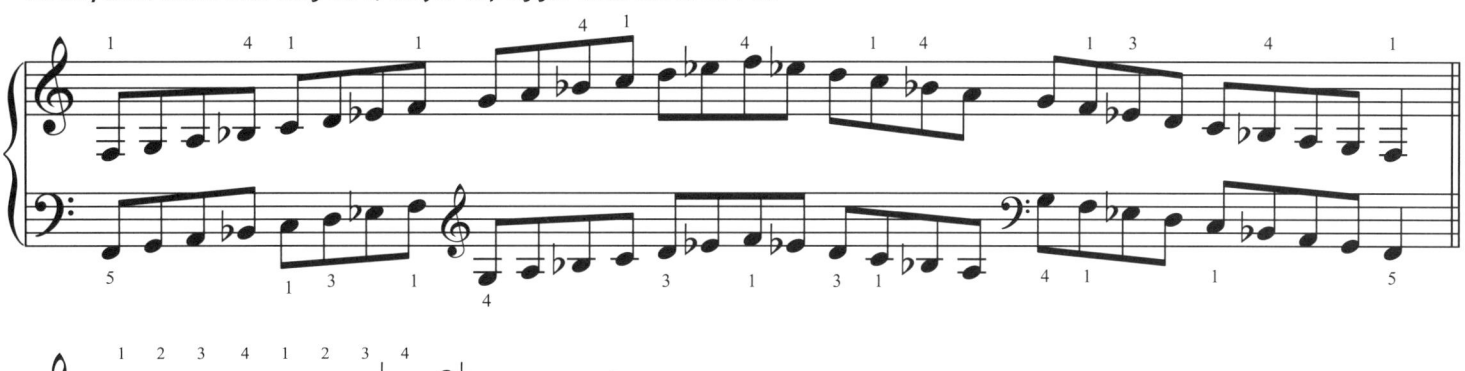

Mixolydian scale starting on D, major arpeggio with lowered 7th

Mixolydian scale starting on D♭, major arpeggio with lowered 7th

F major pentatonic scale (two octaves), straight *and* swung

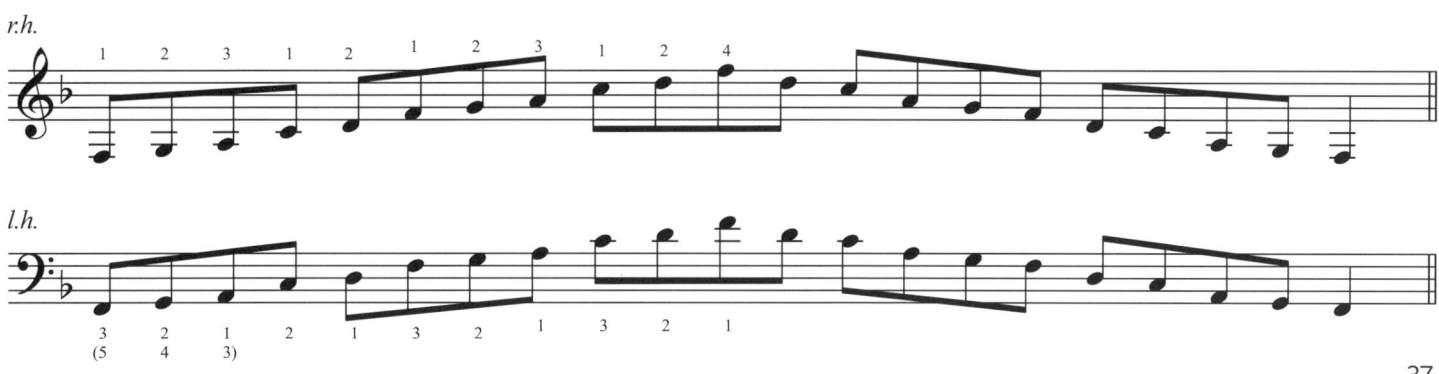

D major pentatonic scale (two octaves), straight *and* swung

D♭ major pentatonic scale (two octaves), straight *and* swung

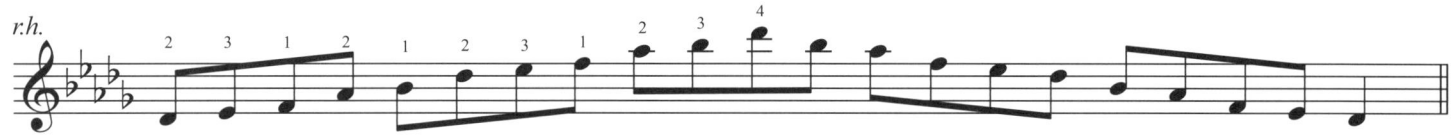

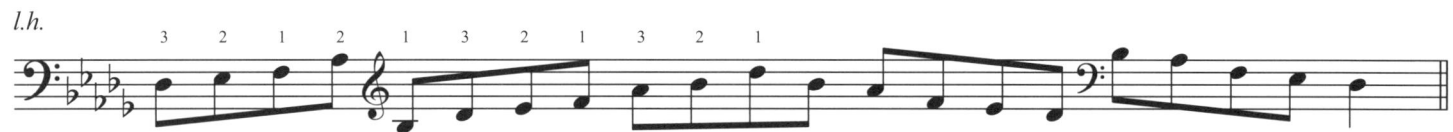

F minor pentatonic scale (two octaves), straight *and* swung

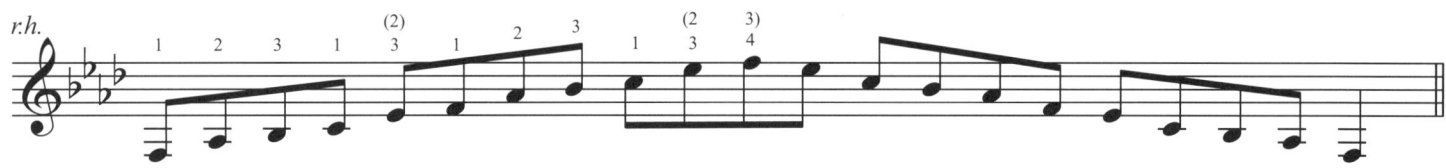

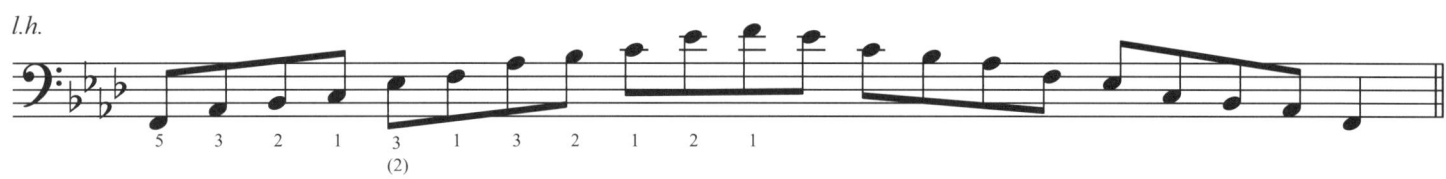

D minor pentatonic scale (two octaves), straight *and* swung

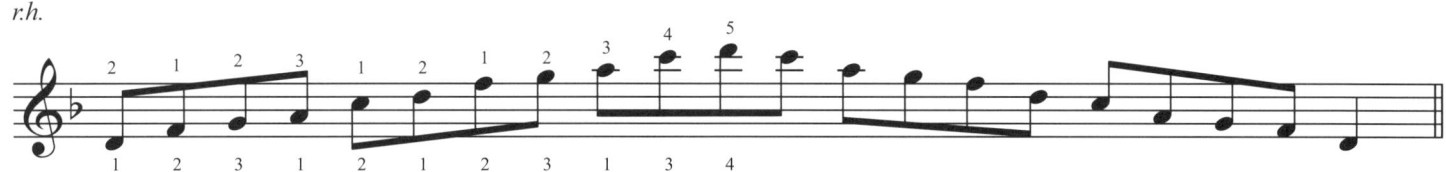

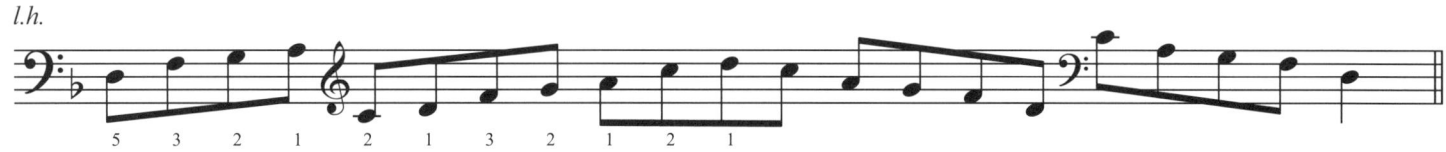

C♯ minor pentatonic scale (two octaves), straight *and* swung

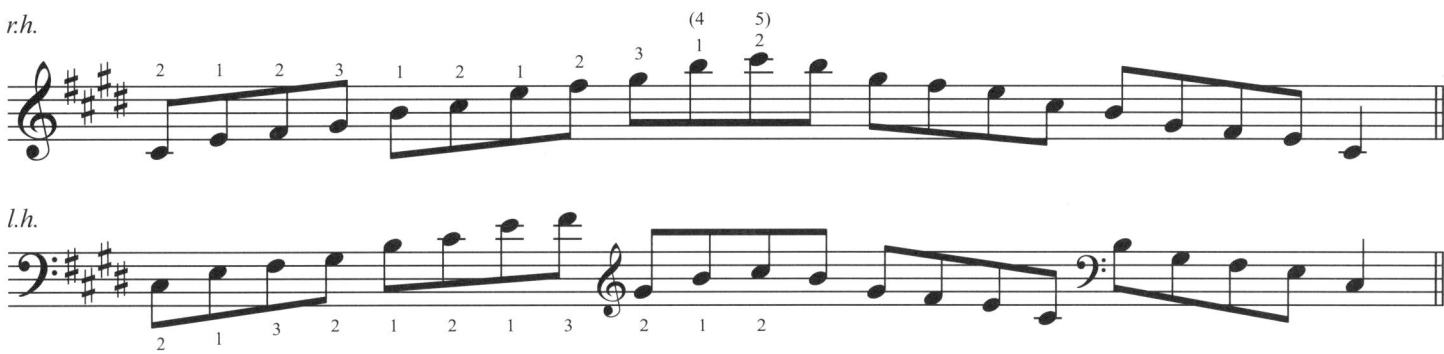

Chromatic scale in similar motion starting on any white note, eg B, (two octaves)

Blues scale on F (two octaves), straight *and* swung

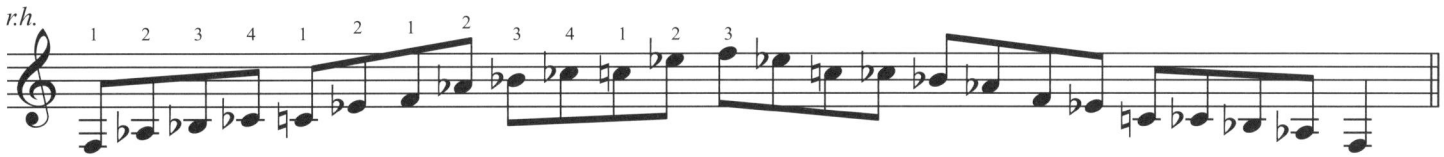

Blues scale on D (two octaves), straight *and* swung

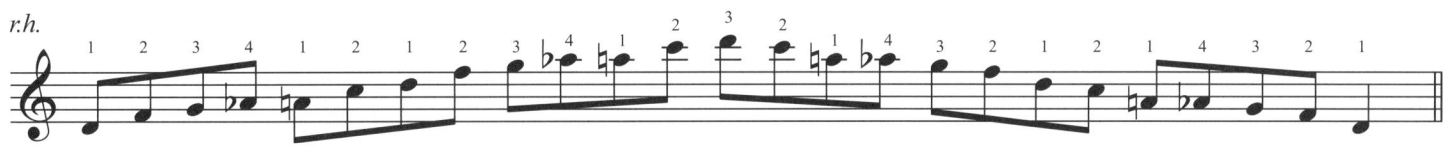

Blues scale on C♯ (two octaves), straight *and* swung

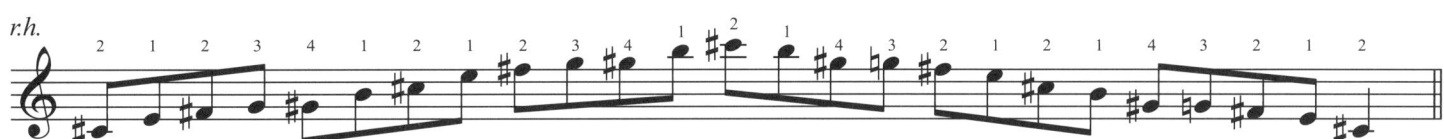

Chords in root position

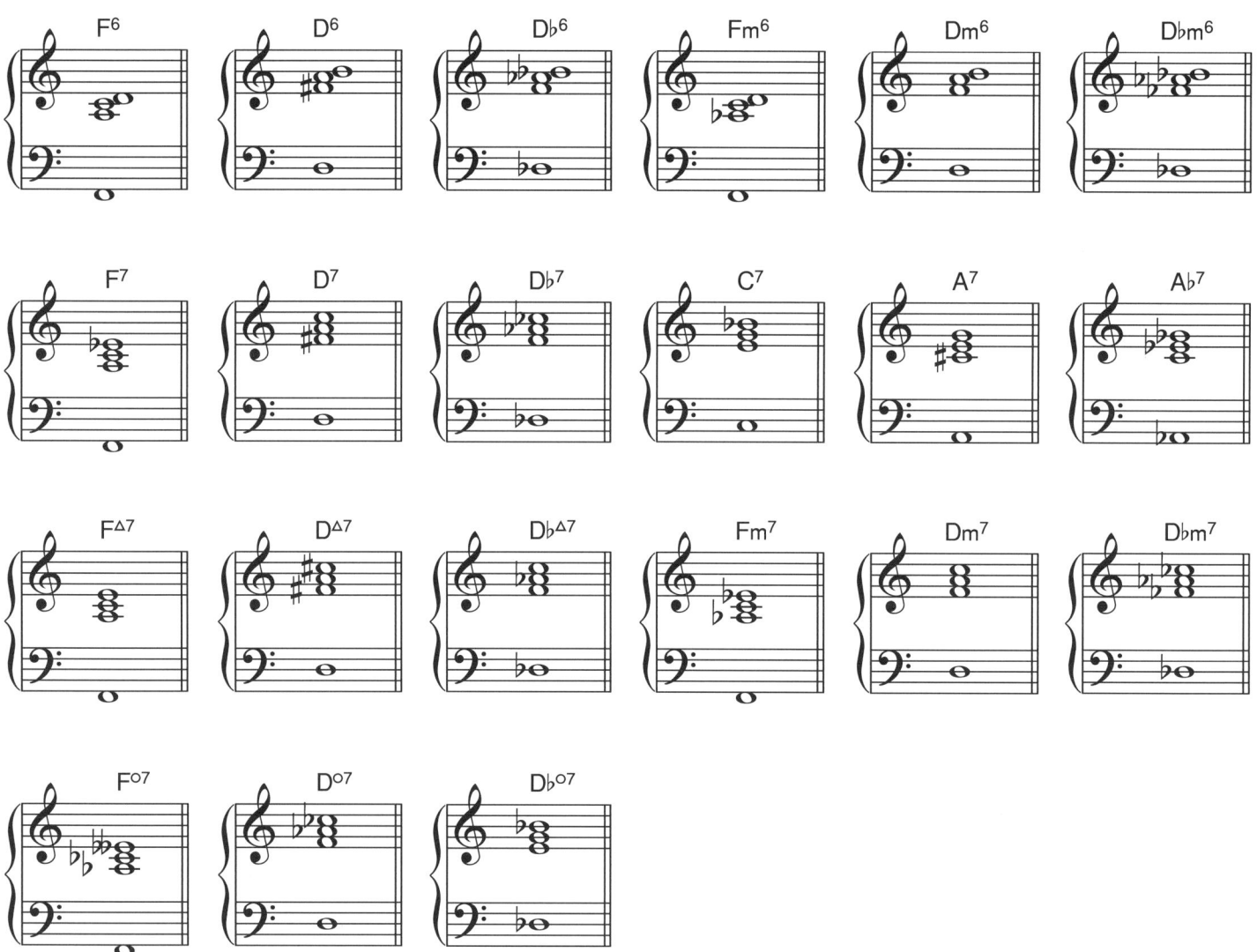

3. Exercises

1. Eastern Song – keyboard functions

Voices: Sheng (or Eastern wind instrument) at sounding pitch, Sitar, Xylophone
Style: 16-beat Oriental style (eg Dangdut)
Other info: Rhythm to be set at low volume

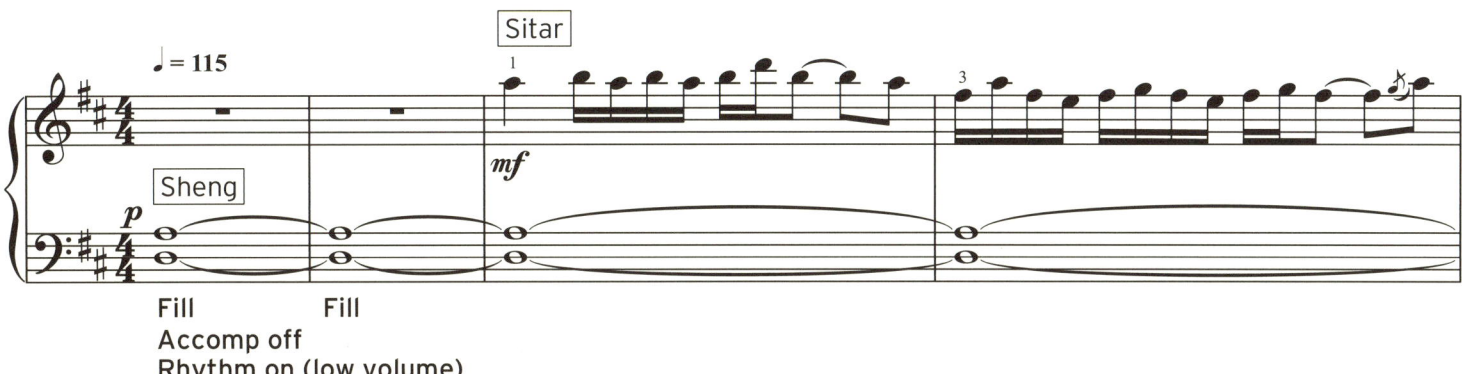

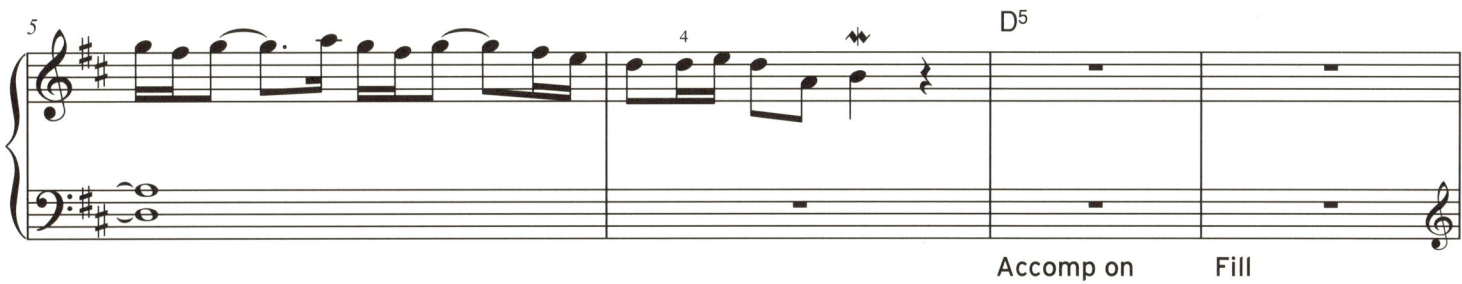

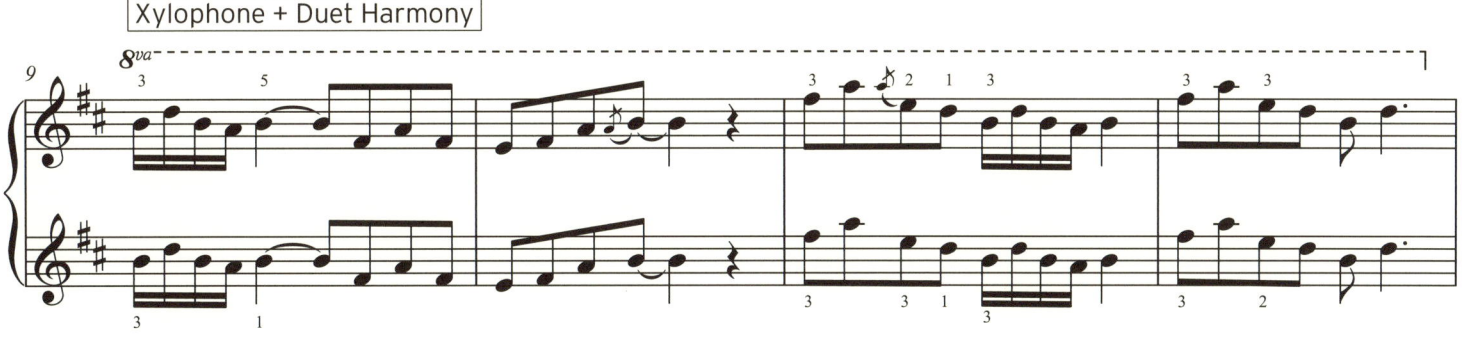

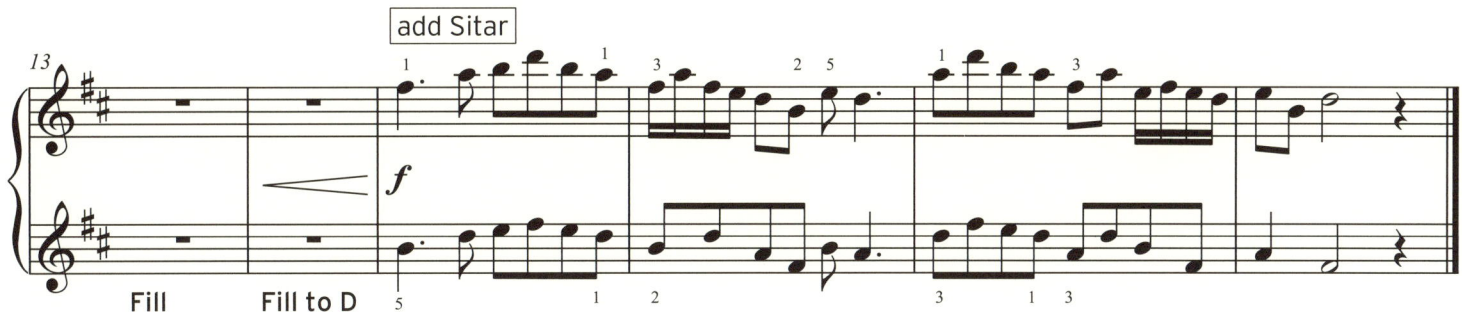

2. Beguine – scalic

> Voice: Flute, Piano
> Style: Beguine

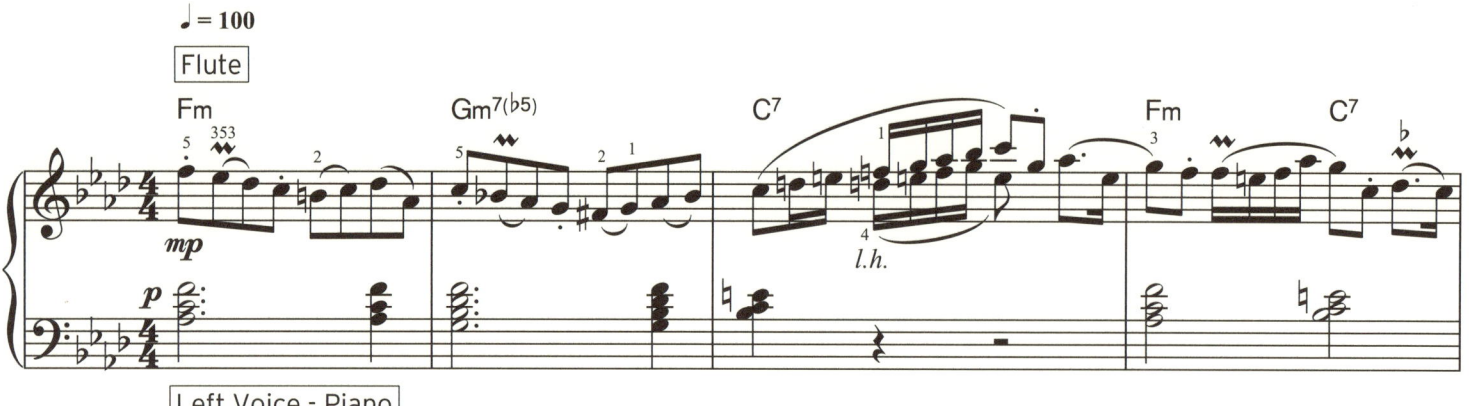

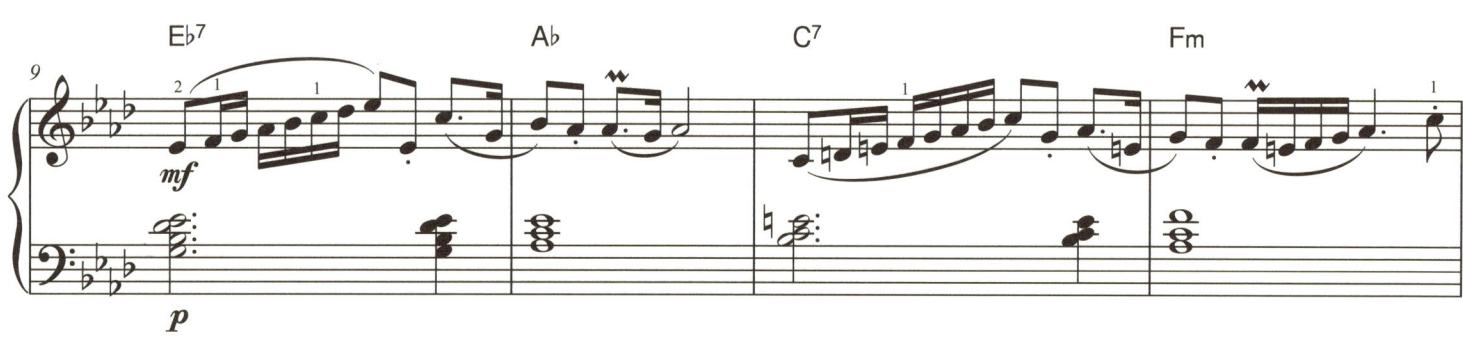
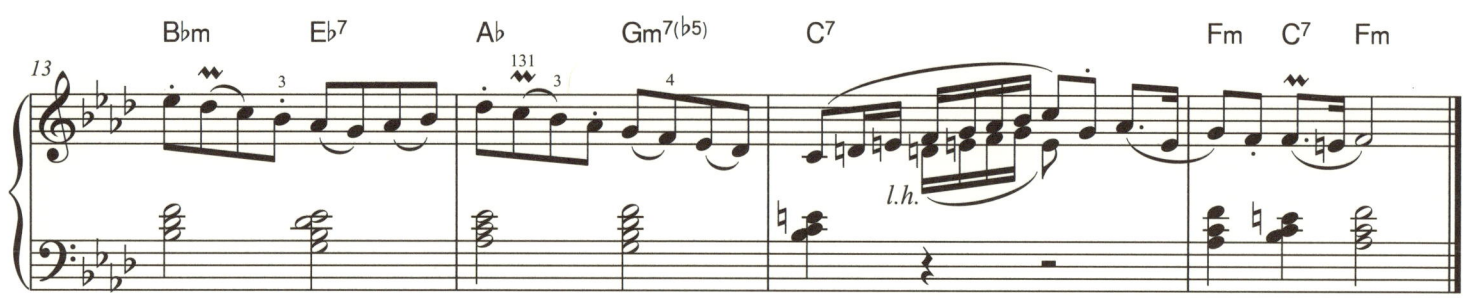

3. Latin Escapade – pianistic

Voices: Classical Guitar (sounding at written pitch), Strings
Style: None

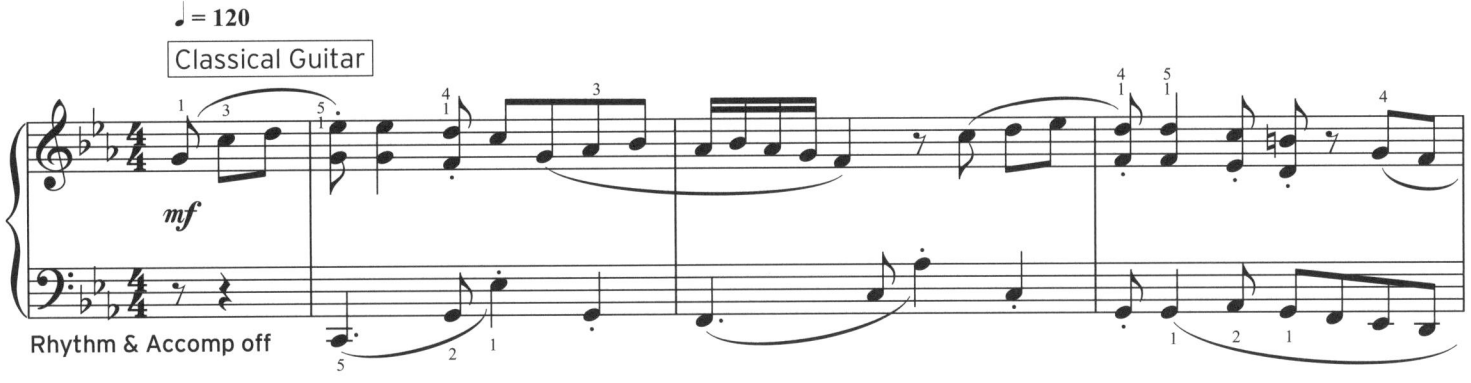

4. Fishes' Lament – sequencing

> Voices: (Clarinet), Electric Piano
> Style: Epic Ballad
> Other info: The volume of the pre-recorded track should be appropriately set so that the live performance is clear.

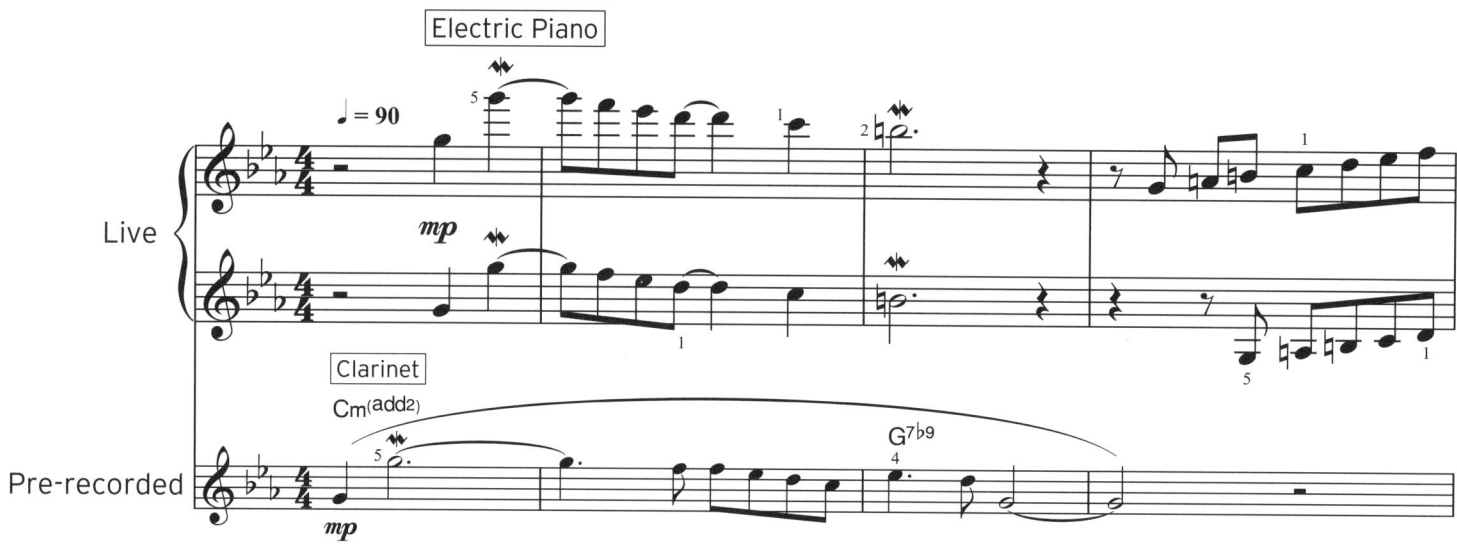

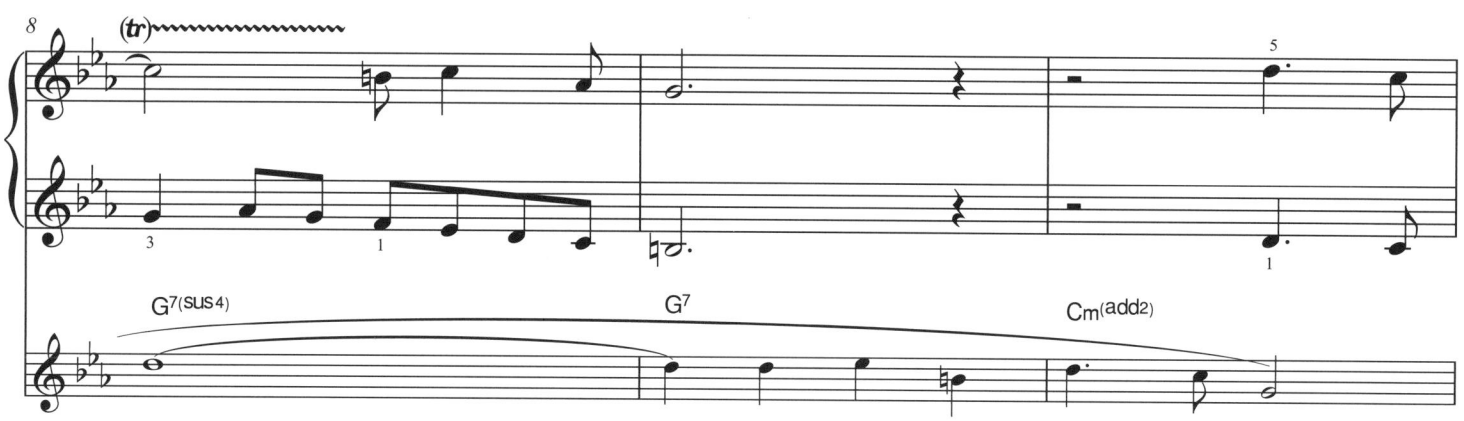